MARTINI

MARTINI

MORE THAN **40** CLASSIC & MODERN RECIPES
FOR THE ICONIC COCKTAIL

DAVID T. SMITH
& KELI RIVERS

Photography by
ALEX LUCK

RYLAND PETERS & SMALL
LONDON • NEW YORK

Senior designer Toni Kay
Production manager
  Gordana Simakovic
Editorial director Julia Charles
Creative director Leslie Harrington
Food stylist Lorna Brash
Prop stylist Luis Peral

Indexer Vanessa Bird

First published in 2023 by
Ryland Peters & Small
20–21 Jockey's Fields
London WC1R 4BW
and
341 E 116th Street
New York, 10029

www.rylandpeters.com

10 9 8 7 6 5 4 3 2 1

Text © David T. Smith & Keli Rivers
2023. Design and photographs
© Ryland Peters & Small 2023.

ISBN: 978-1-78879-512-8

A CIP record for this book is available
from the British Library.
US Library of Congress CIP data
has been applied for.

Printed in China

Author dedications:
To Joe 'J-money' Barber

To Allison and Zahra for
understanding that coupes
must go in the freezer

MIX
Paper | Supporting
responsible forestry
FSC® C008047

CONTENTS

INTRODUCTION

On the face of it, the Martini is perhaps the simplest cocktail there is – to quote Cole Porter, it is simply 'a mixture of gin and vermouth' – however no cocktail has been more scrutinized for the minutiae of how it's made, whether that be the glass, the ratio of ingredients, the garnish, or the method. This book embraces all of these particular peculiarities in an aim to help you make the best Martini you can, to your taste.

TOP TIPS FOR MASTERING MARTINIS

The No1 Tip: Chill!
The one thing you can do to up your Martini game is to chill your glasses beforehand. This can be done by storing them in the freezer for hours (ideal) or by filling the glasses with ice and water before you start mixing and then discarding just before pouring.

Gin or Vodka?
Unless otherwise stated, the recipes in this book are designed to work with almost ANY gin or vodka, although brand recommendations that work particularly well are given. This allows you to customize recipes to the preferences of you/your guests and adapt to whatever spirits are available.

What is 'dry'?
Dryness is a shorthand way to describe the ratio of spirit to vermouth: the less vermouth, the dryer it is. For example, a Martini consisting of 5 parts gin and one part vermouth (5:1) is dryer than one that is 2 parts gin and one part vermouth (2:1). (See also Alternative Martinis, on page 9)

Shaken vs Stirred
There is much debate over shaken vs stirred. Ultimately, it is a matter of personal choice, but there are some notable differences. Stirring produces a crystal-clear drink that is less dilute, can seem boozier and is potentially less cold, but if you stir for long enough (at least 30 seconds), temperature shouldn't be a problem.

Shaking typically results in a colder drink with slightly more dilution and a fluffier texture. This is created by the trapping of air bubbles (aeration), which also gives it a cloudy appearance. Shaking will also create small ice shards, so the drink will need to be fine-strained (with a clean tea strainer) to remove them before serving.

Glassware
While the Martini is typically associated with the V-shaped cocktail glass, it has historically been served in all manner of stemmed glasses: from wine to sherry, coupes to cordial glasses. When it comes to size, less is more. A perfect Martini glass size is 45–90 ml/1½–3 oz., even if the drink doesn't fit; you can always top it up later with any remainder – this is known as 'the dividend'.

How to make a citrus twist
Using a vegetable peeler, peel away a small 2-cm (1-inch) strip of citrus peel. You want mostly zest, not pith. Once the drink is made, hold the peel over the drink between your thumb and second and third fingers. Gently flex it away from you. This causes the aromatic citrus oils to spray out of the peel and settle on the drink's surface.

These tips will help you with whatever Martini you make and hopefully the rest of this book will provide inspiration for numerous delicious drinks and enjoyable social occasions.

ALTERNATIVE MARTINIS

There are a number of different spirits and liqueurs that can be used in a Martini instead of vermouth, which each create a particular variation. You can mix however you'd like, using your preferred ratio and method.

Stone's Ginger Wine –
Cushing Martini

Fino Sherry –
Bone-Dry Martini

Amontillado Sherry –
The Raven

Yellow Chartreuse –
Alaska Martini

Grand Marnier
(with red vermouth) –
The Leap Year

Bitters such as Underberg or Chartreuse Elixir Vegetal can also be used instead of vermouth, albeit sparingly as they are more concentrated in flavour!

CLASSIC

DRY MARTINI

IN THE INTRODUCTION, WE'VE ALREADY DISCUSSED WHAT
MAKES A MARTINI 'DRY', THE RELATIVE BENEFITS OF SHAKING
AND STIRRING, AND THE OLIVE VS. LEMON DEBATE, SO IT'S
NOW TIME FOR A DRINK!

50 ml/1½ oz. Dry Gin or Vodka
10 ml/¼ oz. Dolin Dry Vermouth
Twist of lemon peel or a stuffed olive, to garnish

SERVES 1

Add ingredients to a mixing glass with plenty of ice.
Stir vigorously for at least 60 seconds – it'll be worth
the wait. Strain the drink into a chilled cocktail glass
and garnish with an olive or a twist of lemon peel.

What do you do if you've made too much Martini for
your glass? Simply pour it into a small carafe or jug
and save it for later; this is known as 'the dividend'.

IN & OUT MARTINI

*Some bartenders make an 'In and Out Martini', where
ice is simply coated or rinsed with vermouth. They do this
by pouring some into the ice-filled mixing vessel and then
immediately straining it out again and discarding.*

FIFTY–FIFTY MARTINI

*If you have a special vermouth that you want to taste more
of in your cocktail, try a wetter Martini such as a Fifty-Fifty
Martini (equal parts gin and vermouth) or even a Reverse
Martini, which uses two-thirds vermouth and one-third gin.
This is also known as a 'Julia Childs', named after the
celebrity chef's fondness for them, and works exceptionally
well with a navy-strength gin.*

DIRTY MARTINI

THIS COCKTAIL MADE WITH OLIVE BRINE IS KNOWN AS A DIRTY MARTINI AND WAS INVENTED IN 1901 BY NEW YORK BARTENDER JOHN E. O'CONNOR. IT HAS A DECADENT, VELVETY TEXTURE.

50 ml/1³/₄ oz. Potato Vodka
(such as Royal Mash) or Gin Eva Olive Gin
10 ml/¹/₄ oz. Dry Vermouth
(Vault Coastal is particularly good)
5–15 ml/¹/₄–¹/₂ oz. green olive brine
3 green olives, to garnish

SERVES 1

Muddle 2–3 olives in the bottom of a cocktail shaker, add ice and the vermouth and shake vigorously. Strain into a cocktail glass and garnish with 1 or 3 olives.

You can use any vodka, but potato- or grain-based varieties seem to work best; fruit-based vodkas tend to clash and are usually best avoided.

FILTHY MARTINI

For a Filthy Martini, add another 10–15 ml/¹/₂–³/₄ oz. olive brine to the above recipe. This cocktail has a viscous, oily texture and a real bite of salinity, making it perfect for raising the appetite, but dangerous if you've skipped lunch. It should always be served with some extra olives on the side.

GIBSON MARTINI

For another savoury cocktail try a Gibson Martini, a classic Dry Martini where the only variation is the addition of a small pearl cocktail onion, which adds a delightful touch of 'umami' to the drink.

MARTINI-ON-THE-ROCKS

THE THINKING 'MAN'S' MARTINI, THIS DRINK IS SERVED
IN A TUMBLER AND REPRESENTS THE COCKTAIL'S MORE
CONTEMPLATIVE SIDE.

60 ml/2 oz. Cotswolds Dry Gin
   or a grape-based vodka such as
   Chilgrove or Chapel Down
15 ml/¹/₂ oz. Dry Vermouth
3–4 dashes Orange Bitters
Strip of lemon peel, to garnish (optional)

SERVES 1

Add ingredients to an ice-filled tumbler
and gently stir. Add your preferred garnish,
sit back and enjoy!

*This is a Martini that is meant to be
savoured and the additional ice-melt helps
to lengthen and mellow the drink, as well
as allowing the fragrant orange notes of
the bitters to come through.*

*For a sweeter alternative, try a Gin & It (see
page 23) and, if you can't decide between
sweet and dry, why not try a Perfect Martini?
This splits the vermouth portion of the drink
equally between sweet and dry vermouth.*

DIAMOND MARTINI

ALSO KNOWN AS THE 'FROZEN' OR 'DIRECT' MARTINI, THIS IS HOW MARTINIS ARE FAMOUSLY SERVED AT THE WORLD-RENOWNED DUKES HOTEL IN ST. JAMES, LONDON. THE TECHNIQUE WAS PERFECTED BY SALVATORE CALABRESE IN THE MID-1980S FOR REGULAR PATRON STANTON DELAPLANE, WHO WANTED A VERY, VERY COLD AND VERY, VERY DRY MARTINI.

COOLNESS IS KEY WHEN IT COMES TO THIS DRINK; BOTH THE GLASS AND THE SPIRIT ARE STORED IN THE FREEZER. THE GLASS IS THEN RINSED WITH DRY VERMOUTH OR, FOR A TOUCH OF THE THEATRICS, SPRAYED WITH AN ATOMIZER CONTAINING VERMOUTH.

60 ml/2 oz. chilled Hepple Gin (or other juniper-forward gin) or Smirnoff Blue Vodka
Rinse or spritz of Dry Vermouth

SERVES 1

Pour the chilled spirit directly into the chilled, vermouth-rinsed glass.

This drink has a beautiful purity to it and so many drinkers prefer it 'Dickens' style – that is, without olive or twist!

The low temperature of the spirit increases its viscosity and gives it an indulgent mouthfeel. The higher the ABV, the thicker the texture, but bear in mind that this is essentially a glass of exceptionally cold, neat alcohol, so a spirit at around 45–47% ABV gives just the right balance.

A word of caution: these Martinis can go down extremely easily and quickly due to their low temperature, which is why Dukes Hotel limits visitors to a maximum order of two!

GIMLET

LONG ASSOCIATED WITH THE NAVY, THIS MARTINI VARIATION USES LIME JUICE INSTEAD OF VERMOUTH. PRESERVED LIME JUICE WAS GIVEN TO SAILORS TO HELP PREVENT SCURVY. THE NAME OF THE COCKTAIL MOST LIKELY COMES FROM A TOOL USED TO BORE HOLES IN THE BARRELS IN WHICH THE JUICE WOULD BE STORED.

45 ml/1 1/2 oz. Plymouth Navy Strength Gin or Mermaid Sea Salt Vodka

15 ml/1/2 oz. Rose's Lime Cordial

Twist of lemon and lime peel, to garnish

SERVES 1

Shake with ice and then fine-strain into a coupe or small wine glass. Garnish with peel.

GIMBLET

THIS SLIGHT VARIATION ON A GIMLET IS NAMED AFTER A SWINGING MANOEUVRE THAT WAS USED TO HELP STOW AN ANCHOR AT SEA AND IS A DISTANT COUSIN OF THE DAIQUIRI.

50 ml/1 3/4 oz. Navy Strength Gin

20 ml/2/3 oz. Fresh Lime Juice

10 ml/1/3 oz. Sugar Syrup

Lime wheel, to garnish

SERVES 1

Shake with ice and then fine-strain into a coupe or small wine glass.

LONG GIMLET

For a refreshing variation, make a Gimlet (as above) and dump the entire contents of the shaker (including the ice) into a tall glass. This method is known as 'dirty dumping'. Add more ice, top up with sparkling water and garnish with a mint leaf (optional).

VESPER

A VARIATION THAT FIRST APPEARED IN IAN FLEMING'S FIRST JAMES BOND NOVEL, *CASINO ROYALE*, IN 1953. THE DRINK WAS INVENTED BY FLEMING AND HIS FRIEND IVAR BRYCE. THE ORIGINAL VESPER, WHICH WAS A RUM-BASED FROZEN COCKTAIL, TOOK ITS NAME FROM THE EVENING PRAYERS, VESPERS. UPON TRYING IT MONTHS LATER, FLEMING TURNED OUT TO NOT REALLY LIKE THE DRINK, DESCRIBING IT AS 'UNPALATABLE' IN A LETTER TO THE *MANCHESTER GUARDIAN*.

60 ml/2 oz. Gordon's Gin Travellers' Edition
   (47.3% ABV)
20 ml/²/₃ oz. Grain-based Vodka
10 ml/¹/₃ oz. Kina Lillet (a 50:50 mix
   of Lillet Blanc and China Martini
   is a great substitute)
Twist of lemon peel, to garnish

SERVES 1

Shake the ingredients vigorously with ice. Serve in a pre-chilled champagne goblet garnished with a thin sliver of lemon peel.

Kina Lillet is no longer available and Lillet Blanc, while still working well in a Vesper, is neither as sweet nor as bitter as Kina Lillet. The China Martini (which is quinine-flavoured) noted in the recipe above compensates for that, but you could also use a smaller proportion of another China liqueur.

Bond states that he likes to have a single drink that is 'large and very strong and very cold, and very well-made'. Just one Vesper of an evening is good advice; if it's good enough for 007….

MARTINEZ

AN ANCESTOR OF THE DRY MARTINI THAT WAS, IN TURN,
INSPIRED BY THE MANHATTAN. IN FACT, AN EARLY RECIPE
FROM 1884 DESCRIBES THE MARTINEZ AS 'SAME AS THE
MANHATTAN, ONLY YOU SUBSTITUTE GIN FOR WHISKY'.

50 ml/1¾ oz. Old Tom Gin
(such as Hernö)

25 ml/¾ oz. Dolin Red Vermouth

1 barspoon Luxardo Maraschino
Cherry Liqueur

2–3 dashes Aromatic Bitters

Twist of lemon peel and
a Maraschino cherry, to
garnish (optional)

SERVES 1

Stir the ingredients with ice
and strain into a glass goblet.

*This cocktail is a sweet and
spicy number that allows you
to explore the wide world of red
vermouth. The choice of vermouth
is really important here as it can
completely change the flavour
profile of your drink: from the
deep, bitter richness of Antica
Formula to the herbaceous
and citrusy Dolin Rouge.*

GIN & IT

A GIN & IT MAKES A LOVELY PRE-DINNER DRINK. THE
OPTIONAL DASH OF WATER TURNS THIS FROM AN EVENING
DRINK TO A SIPPABLE AFTERNOON LIBATION.

50 ml/1½ oz. Classic Dry Gin such
as Brighton Gin or Seagram's

50 ml/1½ oz. Martini Rosso
Red Vermouth

20 ml/¾ oz. Chilled Still or Sparkling
Water (optional)

Long strip of orange peel, to garnish

SERVES 1

Add the ingredients to an
ice-filled glass and serve with
a swizzle stick and a long
slice of orange peel.

CONTEMPORARY

ESPRESSO MARTINI

THE ESPRESSO MARTINI IS ONE OF THE MOST POPULAR
COCKTAILS OF THE LAST FEW YEARS. IT WAS CREATED
BY DICK BRADSELL IN LONDON IN THE 1980S.

45 ml/1 1/2 oz. Beluga Vodka
15 ml/1/2 oz. Conker Coffee Liqueur
30 ml/1 oz. Espresso Coffee (freshly-made)
10 ml/1/4 oz. Simple Syrup
3 espresso beans, to garnish

SERVES 1

Add the ingredients to a cocktail shaker and
shake vigorously with ice. Fine-strain into a
V-shaped cocktail glass. Garnish by floating the
three coffee beans on the surface of the drink.

CORVETTE MARTINI

*A recipe created by Steph DiCamillo of Cocktails
By Mail, this variation adds some aged, woody
elements to the drink. It is made using the
above recipe, but substituting the vodka for
Irish whiskey and the sugar syrup for Drambule
whisky liqueur. Serve it on the rocks for
a delightful evening sipper.*

THE PINK GIN UP

A VARIATION ON A PINK GIN: A CLASSIC NAVAL DRINK
CONTAINING ANGOSTURA BITTERS, WHICH WERE
PRESCRIBED TO HELP SAILORS WITH SEASICKNESS.

50 ml/1¾ oz. Dry Gin
(you could use vodka
if you really wanted to)
10 ml/¼ oz. Dry Vermouth
3–4 dashes Angostura Bitters

SERVES 1

Mix (see notes below) and strain
into a chilled cocktail glass.

*Here the mixing method really does
make a difference: stirring it creates
an incredibly clean and crisp drink
with a delightful balance of spirit and
spice, while shaking creates a fluffy
and aerated drink. The Diamond
Martini method (page 16) could also
be used, with the Angostura Bitters
simply sprinkled around the chilled
glass before pouring the gin in.*

SMOKY MARTINI

THERE ARE A FEW VARIATIONS ON THIS COCKTAIL; SOME OMIT
VERMOUTH AND REPLACE IT WITH ANY OLD SCOTCH WHISKY,
BUT KEEPING IT DOES CREATE A MORE NUANCED DRINK.

A splash of smoky whisky
50 ml/1¾ oz. Volstead's Folly
Gin (the robustness
of many American
gins complement the
smoke well)
10 ml/¼ oz. Dry Vermouth
Flamed orange peel, to
garnish (optional)

SERVES 1

Rinse a chilled glass with a smoky
whisky or use a small atomiser to spray
the glass. Pour in your mixed Martini
(shaken or stirred) and garnish with
a flamed orange peel, if liked.

*Lagavulin 16 is the ultimate whisky for
this drink (a small bottle will last for ages
because you use so little), but Johnnie
Walker Black, Laphroaig or Famous
Grouse Smoky Black also work well.*

PORN STAR MARTINI

A NEW BREED OF MARTINI THAT MOVES BEYOND THE TRADITIONAL MIX OF SPIRIT AND VERMOUTH. WHILE TRADITIONALISTS MAY RAISE AN EYEBROW AT THEIR INCLUSION HERE, THEIR PLACE (AT LEAST IN THE EXTENDED) MARTINI FAMILY IS NOW FIRMLY ESTABLISHED.

60 ml/2 oz. Adnams East Coast Barley Vodka

15 ml/½ oz. Passion Fruit Purée or Passoa Liqueur

15 ml/½ oz. Vanilla Syrup

15 ml/½ oz. Lime Juice

45 ml/1½ oz. Prosecco (chilled)

Slice of passion fruit, to garnish

SERVES 1

Add the ingredients, except for the Prosecco, to an ice-filled shaker and shake vigorously. Fine-strain into a coupe glass and float a slice of passion fruit on top. Serve the chilled Prosecco on the side in another small glass.

RISING STAR MARTINI

A LONGER VERSION OF THE PORN STAR MARTINI WITHOUT THE SIDECAR OF CHILLED PROSECCO.

30 ml/1 oz. Vodka

15 ml/½ oz. Passion Fruit Purée or Passoa Liqueur

15 ml/½ oz. Vanilla Syrup

15 ml/½ oz. Lime Juice

Sparkling Water, to top up

Orange wedge, to garnish

SERVES 1

Add the ingredients to a tall ice-filled glass and stir. Top up with sparkling water and garnish with an orange wedge.

LEGGERO MARTINI

A CREATION OF SAM CARTER OF BOMBAY SAPPHIRE, THIS
COCKTAIL IS A HYBRID OF THE MARTINI AND THE GIN & TONIC.

35 ml/1 1/4 oz. **Bombay
Sapphire Gin**

35 ml/1 1/4 oz. **Martini Bianco
Vermouth**

35 ml/1 1/4 oz. **Fever-Tree
Mediterranean Tonic**

Twist of citrus peel, to garnish

SERVES 1

Add the ingredients, including the
tonic water, to an ice-filled wine
glass and gently stir. Garnish with
a citrus twist.

*If vodka is more to your taste, simply
substitute the gin for a clean, grain-
based vodka such as Grey Goose
and garnish with lime (as shown).*

IMPROVED APPLETINI

A 21ST-CENTURY VERSION OF THE DAY-GLO DISCO DRINK OF
THE 1990S; THIS REMOVES THE RADIOACTIVE COLOUR, BUT
ENHANCES THE FLAVOUR.

50 ml/1 3/4 oz. **Four Pillars
Rare Dry Gin or Grain-
based Vodka**

25 ml/3/4 oz. **Avallen Calvados**

10 ml/1/4 oz. **Orange Liqueur**

**Slice of green apple, to
garnish**

SERVES 1

Add the ingredients to a cocktail
shaker and shake vigorously with ice.
Fine-strain into a coupe glass and
garnish with an apple slice.

*Calvados is an aged apple brandy
(sometimes also containing pear spirit)
from the north of France. It has a rich,
fruity quality with a notable crispness
from the apple. In the United States,
a good-quality applejack would
be a suitable alternative.*

1980'S COSMOPOLITAN

WHEN PEOPLE THINK OF THE 'COSMO', THEY THINK OF THE 1990S – FAME, FASHION AND LIFE IN THE METROPOLIS, BUT THE DRINK GOES BACK NEARLY A CENTURY. THE BEST KNOWN VERSION TODAY WAS PERFECTED BY DALE DEGROFF WHILE HE WAS WORKING AT THE RAINBOW ROOM IN NEW YORK CITY.

45 ml/1 1/2 oz. Hven Vodka
20 ml/1 oz. Cointreau
30 ml/1 1/4 oz. Cranberry Juice
10 ml/1/4 oz. Fresh Lime Juice
Lime wedge, to garnish

SERVES I

Add the ingredients to a cocktail shaker and shake vigorously with ice. Fine-strain into a deep V-shaped glass and garnish with a small wedge of lime.

1930'S COSMOPOLITAN

THERE IS A GIN-BASED PREDECESSOR TO THE COSMOPOLITAN IN THE 1934 BOOK, 'PIONEERS OF MIXING AT ELITE BARS', WHICH USES RASPBERRY SYRUP INSTEAD OF CRANBERRY.

50 ml/1 3/4 oz. Hven Dry Gin
15 ml/1/2 oz. Cointreau
15 ml/1/2 oz. Fresh Lemon Juice
10 ml/1/4 oz. Raspberry Syrup
** or Liqueur**
Twist of lemon peel, to garnish

SERVES I

Add the ingredients to a cocktail shaker and shake vigorously with ice. Strain into a coupe glass and garnish with a small twist of lemon peel

BREAKFAST MARTINI

MANY READERS MAY BAULK AT THE IDEA OF AN EARLY-MORNING MARTINI, BUT THIS DRINK WAS INSPIRED BY THE FLAVOURS OF THE MOST IMPORTANT MEAL OF THE DAY, RATHER THAN BEING DESIGNED TO ACCOMPANY IT.

60 ml/2 oz. Shortcross Gin
15 ml/1/2 oz. Lemon Juice
1 heaped teaspoon Marmalade

SERVES 1

Add the ingredients to a cocktail shaker and shake vigorously with ice. Fine-strain into a V-shaped cocktail glass.

NEW-MAKE MILLIE

NEW-MAKE SPIRIT HAS A COMPLEX BREADY FLAVOUR, A GREAT COMPLEMENT HERE FOR THE MARMALADE.

60 ml/2 oz. New-Make Spirit
  or White Whiskey
15 ml/1/2 oz. Lemon Juice
2 heaped teaspoons Marmalade
Shortbread fingers, to garnish
  (optional)

SERVES 1

Add the ingredients to a cocktail shaker and shake vigorously with ice. Fine-strain into a V-shaped cocktail glass and garnish with a shortbread finger on the side.

New-make spirit is essentially whisky before it is aged. Depending upon the grains and yeast used, the flavours can vary greatly. Holyrood Distillery in Edinburgh produces a wide range of new-make spirits; their Chocolate Malt works particularly well in this cocktail.

EXPERIMENTAL

THE SAINT

ONE OF THE FINEST WAYS TO ENJOY A MARTINI IS
WHILE TRAVELLING; IMAGINE GLIDING ACROSS THE
CLOUDS DURING A TRANSATLANTIC CROSSING TO THE
UNITED STATES. THAT IS EXACTLY WHAT PASSENGERS,
INCLUDING NOVELIST LESLIE CHARTELIS AND HIS WIFE
PAULINE, EXPERIENCED ON THE 1930'S AIRSHIP, THE
HINDENBURG. THE AIRSHIP WAS SUPPLIED FOR GERMAN
TASTES OF THE DAY AND AS A RESULT ONCE RAN OUT OF
GIN, SO MRS. CHARTELIS SUGGESTED USING KIRSCHWASSER
FOR MARTINIS INSTEAD.

45 ml/1½ oz. Kirschwasser
   or other Cherry Eau de Vie

15 ml/½ oz. Dry Vermouth

2–3 dashes Chocolate Bitters
   (an optional addition for the 21st century)

Cocktail cherry, to garnish (optional)

SERVES 1

Shake vigorously with ice and strain into a chilled
cocktail glass. Leave ungarnished or, for a striking
accompaniment, add a cocktail cherry.

*The 3:1 ratio used here is typical of Dry Martinis
from the 1930s and the shaken method gives the
drink a fluffy, cloud-like texture – very suitable when
cruising 220 metres/720 feet above sea level!*

GT TURBO

A COMPRESSED GIN & TONIC CREATED BY TRISTAN
STEPHENSON AND THOMAS ASKE AT THEIR LONDON
BAR, PURL, IN 2010.

60 ml/2 oz. Hayman's London Dry Gin
(or other classic gin)

10 ml/¼ oz. Fresh Lime Juice

10 ml/¼ oz. Tonic Water Syrup
(commercial or home-made, see below)

2–3 dashes Orange Bitters

Lime wheel, to garnish (optional)

SERVES 1

Add the ingredients to a cocktail shaker and
shake vigorously with ice. Fine-strain into a
V-shaped cocktail glass.

To make the tonic water syrup:
Add 250 ml/1 cup bottled tonic water (this
is a great way to use up tonic water that has
gone flat) and heat over a medium heat. The
water will gradually evaporate, leaving the
tonic syrup. When the volume of the liquid has
roughly halved, remove the pan from the heat
and allow the mixture to cool. Store the syrup
in a clean, refrigerated, airtight bottle for
up to 2 weeks.

GARDEN GIN GRANITA

PART-DESSERT AND PART-DRINK, A GRANITA IS SIMILAR TO A SORBET, BUT HAS A MORE FLAKY TEXTURE AS IT IS SCRAPED TOGETHER DURING THE FREEZING PROCESS. THE GREAT THING ABOUT IT IS THAT IT NEEDS NO SPECIAL EQUIPMENT TO MAKE: JUST A BOWL AND A FREEZER.

120 ml/4 oz. Juniper-forward Gin

120 ml/4 oz. Dry Vermouth or even dry white wine

200 ml/6¾ oz. Fresh Grapefruit Juice
(freshly squeezed makes all the difference)

3 pinches of kosher salt/salt flakes

Sparkling Water, to top up

Grated pink grapefruit zest and/or mint leaves,
to garnish

SERVES 6–8

Mix all the ingredients together the night before in a shallow metal dish and place in the freezer overnight. Then use a fork to scrape the granita into a snow-like consistency.

To serve, add one scoop to a large margarita glass and top up with sparkling wine. Serve at once garnished with grated pink grapefruit and/or a fresh mint leaf.

RUMTINI

THIS MARTINI VARIATION SIMPLY USES UNAGED RUM INSTEAD OF GIN OR VODKA. YOU CAN USE YOUR OWN PREFERRED RATIO OF RUM TO VERMOUTH AND MIX IT HOWEVER YOU LIKE, ALTHOUGH STIRRING IS OFTEN MORE SYMPATHETIC TO THE RUM'S UNDERLYING CHARACTER.

**50 ml/1³/₄ oz. Unaged Rum
(the grassiness of Portsmouth
Distillery's 1968 Rum
is particularly tasty)**

10 ml/¹/₂ oz. Dry Vermouth

**Twist of lime peel and grated
nutmeg, to garnish (optional)**

SERVES 1

Stir ingredients in a mixing glass with ice before straining into a small, stemmed wine glass. Garnish with a twist of lime peel and a pinch of grated nutmeg.

SPICE ISLAND

THIS DRINK PAIRS THE DEEP COMPLEXITY OF RED VERMOUTH AND SPICED RUM WITH THE WOODY NOTES OF AGED RUM.

**30 ml/1 oz. Merser Signature
Rum or other Aged Rum**

10 ml/¹/₂ oz. Red Vermouth

**10 ml /¹/₂ oz. Cinnabar or other
Spiced Rum**

Twist of orange peel, to garnish

SERVES 1

Add the ingredients to a cocktail shaker and shake vigorously with ice. Strain into a tall, stemmed glass and garnish with a twist of orange peel.

DRY MANHATTAN

THE MANHATTAN IS AN ANCESTOR OF THE MARTINI THAT IS COMMONLY MIXED WITH RED VERMOUTH; THIS PLEASING VARIATION IS INSPIRED BY THE MID-CENTURY TREND FOR DRYNESS IN A MARTINI.

50 ml/1½ oz. Rye Whiskey
   (such as Jim Beam)
10 ml/½ oz. Dry Vermouth
2-3 dashes Orange Bitters
Twist of lemon peel, to garnish

SERVES I

Add the ingredients to a mixing glass and stir. Strain into a stemmed cocktail glass and garnish with a twist of lemon.

CLEOPATRA

WHILE THE EGYPTIAN QUEEN FAMOUSLY BATHED IN ASSES' MILK, ORDINARY COW'S MILK IS BETTER FOR THIS DRINK (OAT MILK WORKS, TOO).

30 ml/1 oz. Bourbon
20 ml/½ oz. Sweet Vermouth
50 ml/1½ oz. Semi-skimmed Milk
   (or Oat Milk)
10 ml/¼ oz. Luxardo Maraschino
   Cherry Liqueur

SERVES I

Add the ingredients with ice to a cocktail shaker and shake vigorously. Fine-strain into a stemmed cocktail glass.

HIGH-RISE MARTINI

MARTINIS ARE OFTEN SHORT AND POTENT, BUT ON A
HOT SUMMER'S DAY IT CAN BE NICE TO HAVE THE TASTE
OF A MARTINI IN A DRINK THAT IS MORE REFRESHING
AND THIRST-QUENCHING.

**30 ml/1 oz. Mermaid Zesty Citrus Gin
or Adnams Rye Vodka**

1 barspoon Dry Vermouth

1 barspoon Bianco Vermouth

**100 ml/3¼ oz. Sparkling Water or Sparkling
Lemonade or even Cola for a sweeter drink**

Lemon, lime and orange peel, to garnish

SERVES 1

Add the alcohols to an ice-filled highball
glass (spirit first) and give the drink a
gentle stir. Top up with your mixer of
choice and garnish with a lemon,
lime and orange peel.

MAR-TEA-NI

PUNS ASIDE, TEA IS AN EXCELLENT AND OFTEN UNDER-UTILIZED COCKTAIL INGREDIENT. IT GOES PARTICULARLY WELL WITH GIN AND, WITH A VAST RANGE READILY AVAILABLE, YOUR CREATIVITY CAN KNOW NO LIMITS.

50 ml/1¾ oz. Gin or Vodka
10 ml/½ oz. Lillet Blanc (or Bianco Vermouth)
Tea bag of your choice

SERVES 1

Infuse the tea bag in your spirit for 60–90 seconds and then stir with vermouth over ice. Strain into an ice-filled glass teacup.

This drink allows a lot of room for innovation, as the tea that you use makes a massive difference to the cocktail. English Breakfast tea is a great starting point. Peppermint adds a cool mint freshness, as well as some sweet, hay-like qualities. Earl Grey brings more floral flavours of bergamot and citrus, and Lapsang Souchong brings an elegant smokiness – just make sure you don't leave the tea bag in too long!

SEASONAL

FASCINATOR

SPRING IS A TIME FOR NEW LIFE AND
FLORAL BLOSSOMS, WHETHER THAT BE
JAPANESE CHERRY BLOSSOM (SAKURA) OR
THE MORE DOMESTIC ELDERFLOWER. THIS
DRINK PRESENTS BOTH, IN A DELICIOUS WAY.

45 ml/1½ oz. Japanese Gin (such as Roku)

20 ml/¾ oz. Mancino Sakura Vermouth
   (or Dry Vermouth)

1 barspoon Elderflower Cordial

2–3 dashes Absinthe

Mint leaves, to garnish

SERVES 1

Add the ingredients to a mixing glass and
stir with ice. Strain into a chilled coupe glass
and garnish with a few mint leaves.

SWEETHEART MARTINI

A ROMANTIC COCKTAIL THAT'S PERFECT FOR VALENTINE'S DAY, AN ANNIVERSARY, OR A SPECIAL DATE NIGHT, WHICH OF COURSE MEANS THIS RECIPE SERVES TWO.

60 ml/2 oz. Dry Gin (ideally floral-forward, such as Silent Pool) or Vodka (milk-based; Blacklion is particularly good)

15 ml/½ oz. Fresh Lemon Juice

15 ml/½ oz. Rose Honey or Rose Liqueur

Sparkling Rosé Wine, chilled, to top up

Rose petals, to garnish (fresh or dried, but always food safe)

SERVES 2

Add all the ingredients, except the wine, to a cocktail shaker and shake vigorously with ice. Strain and split the contents between 2 glasses, before topping up with the sparkling wine. Garnish each drink with a rose petal.

MR BLUE SKY

AN EYE-CATCHING AND FUN COCKTAIL, PERFECT FOR
SUMMER FESTIVITIES. THE DRINK IS A STARTLING SHADE
OF BLUE AND GARNISHED WITH A SINGLE, LONELY CLOUD.

45 ml/1½ oz. Citadelle Jardin d'Été
 (or other citrusy Dry Gin)
20 ml/½ oz. Martini Bianco Vermouth
 (or other Sweet White Vermouth)
10 ml/¼ oz. Blue Curaçao
10 ml/¼ oz. Fresh Lemon Juice
Candy floss/cotton candy, to garnish

SERVES 1

Add the ingredients to a cocktail shaker and
shake vigorously with ice. Fine-strain into a
classic V-shaped cocktail glass and garnish
with a little puff of candy floss – ideally white
or blue, but pink works, too. For those who
would like a sweeter drink, simply add some
of the candy floss to the drink.

*For a vodka-based alternative, replace the gin
with a citrus-flavoured vodka (St. George Spirits'
California Citrus is an excellent choice).*

REMEMBER ME MARTINI

AUTUMN/FALL IS A CONTEMPLATIVE SEASON THAT PERHAPS
DESERVES A THOUGHTFUL MARTINI, SO THIS DRINK HAS
HINTS OF SMOKE AND A GENTLE WARMTH FROM CHILLI.

40 ml/1½ oz. Blanco Mezcal (or Tequila)

15 ml/½ oz. Martini Bianco Vermouth
(or other Sweet White Vermouth)

15 ml/½ oz. Ancho Reyes Verde Chile Liqueur
(or other Chilli Liqueur)

10 ml/¼ oz. Lime Juice

Green olive and a cocktail gherkin, to garnish

SERVES 1

Add the ingredients to a cocktail shaker
and shake vigorously with ice. Fine-strain
into a small margarita glass and garnish
with an olive and a cocktail gherkin.

*The drink calls for Ancho Reyes Verde Chile
Liqueur, which was first made in Mexico in
1927. It is made using ancho and roasted
poblano chilli peppers and the result is
a balanced, but accessible product that
won't blow your head off, but makes a
deliciously spicy Margarita.*

THE COUNTESS' KISS

A MONSTER MARTINI FOR THE SPOOKY SEASON THAT
IS HALLOWEEN... THE GRAPEFRUIT PEEL FANGS ARE
OPTIONAL BUT ADD A PLEASINGLY THEATRICAL TOUCH.

40 ml/2 oz. Reposado Tequila
20 ml/1 oz. Amontillado Sherry
20 ml/1 oz. Blood Orange Juice
15 ml/³/₄ oz. Sugar Syrup
Grapefruit peel fangs, to garnish (optional)

SERVES 1

Add the ingredients to a cocktail shaker and
shake vigorously with ice. Fine strain into a
coupe glass and garnish with grapefruit fangs.

To make the grapefruit peel fangs:
Use a vegetable peeler to peel a large piece
of grapefruit peel (approx. 4 x 7 cm/1 ¹/₂ x 2³/₄
inches). On a chopping board, use a sharp
knife to carefully cut a jagged zig-zag to
form the fangs on one end.

*Amontillado sherry is ideal for this cocktail
and was a favourite of horror writer Edgar Allen
Poe. Cream or sweet sherry also works, but you
may want to omit the additional sugar syrup.*

HOT SPICED-TINI

A COSY WINTER WARMER SERVED IN A LARGE BRANDY BALLOON THAT YOU CAN CRADLE IN YOUR HANDS ON A COLD WINTER'S NIGHT.

50 ml/1³/₄ oz. Aged Gin (Booth's or Campfire are both good choices)

20 ml/¹/₂ oz. Montenegro Amaro

10 ml/¹/₄ oz. Red Vermouth (Sacred English Spiced is ideal)

3–4 dashes Angostura Bitters

60 ml/2 oz. Hot Water (not boiling)

Orange peel and a star of anise, to garnish

SERVES I

Preheat a brandy balloon with warm water (hot tap water is fine). Add all the ingredients to a heat-proof jug/pitcher and stir without ice, then gently pour the mix into the brandy balloon before garnishing with a piece of orange peel and a star of anise.

THE MILLIONAIRE'S MARTINI

A DECADENT MARTINI WITH A DAZZLING GARNISH
TO SEE THE OLD YEAR OUT AND THE NEW YEAR IN.

**50 ml/1¾ oz. Beefeater Crown Jewel Dry Gin
or Grain-based Vodka**

10 ml/¼ oz. Dry Vermouth (such as Dolin)

**A splash of Chilled Dry Sparkling Wine
(Champagne or English Sparkling)**

**Small cocktail sparkler anchored by a roll
of grapefruit peel, to garnish**

SERVES 1

Shake or stir the spirit and vermouth with
ice and then fine-strain into a Champagne
saucer and top up with the sparkling wine.

Garnish with a small cocktail sparkler
anchored by a roll of grapefruit peel.

Caution: make sure to remove the sparkler
before drinking!

*The grapefruit flavours from the Beefeater
Crown Jewel provides a lively zestiness that
pairs well with the dry flavours of the wines,
while the slightly higher ABV gives the drink
a botanical power that is perfect for seeing
the new year in.*

INDEX

ACKNOWLEDGEMENTS

The authors wish to thank Blue Room, Gin Archive, Scruff, Gin Genies, Pal & The Gin Guild, Anita, Beth & Gin Magazine, World Drink Awards, IWSC, Spirits Business, The New Sheridan Club, Bramble Bar, JP Smith, DWS, Dot, Big T & Queenie, The Millers, Big Bad Bernie P & Dr. Damo, Rosie the Bear, Aaron 'AK' Knoll, VK Karlova, VP Piromalo, Julesy, (Also) Becky, GinMonkey, 'M', Camillie, IL Fleming, Ivar Bryce, Dick Bradsell, Jake Burger, Sam Carter, Ian Hart, Lorro, SJ & Rex, Sarah 'Ding Ding' Miller, GinMiller, Bill & Erik Owens and the ADI, Simon & Ali Hartley, Artemis Scarheart, BevFluencers, Sir Roger Moore, Jon Hillgren, Barnaby Conrad III, EZ, DAB, C-Max, SG1, Stevie B, C-Dog, MJ, Sarah Mitchell, Uncie Des, Adam Smithson, The Haymans, Nicholas Cook, Sean Harrison, Seb HM, Craig Harper, Martin Miller, Dimple, Su-Lin, Natasha & The Gin Room, 'The Glasses', Petey-Boy, Scottish Jamie, Geraldine, Steph & Freddy, Peter Cushing, Tristan Stephenson, Jared Brown & Anistatia Miller, Massimiliano Prili, Alessandro Palazzi, Stevo Kennard, Merchant House, Keens, Sarah from Henry's Bar, Nick Ravenhall, Lottie, Jo Alkins, Ben & Kate, Lexy Gabriel, Jaye, Ian W, John McCarthy, Graphic Bar, Duke's Hotel, Purl, Michelle and Jim Rivers, Sally & Andrew, Muddy Rivers, Uncle Ken, Down & Out Bar, Bar Goto, Brooklyn's Trad Room, Milady's, The Attic, UnderCote, Travel Bar, every bartender at Hotsy, Totsy, Donkey's and Grif, Amanda S and her parents, Kellie Thorn, Robin & Jason, Maritza & Ben, Josh, Haley, all my swans JP 'Twist & Olive', Steph 'Blue Cheese Stuffed', Mo 'MusicMan', Molli 'VJOP' & the team at RPS.